KUNG FU FOR YOUNG PEOPLE

An Introduction to Karate and Kung Fu

by Ted Mancuso and Frank Hill

Edited by Gregory Lee
Art Director, Karen Massad

© 1982 by Ted Mancuso and Frank Hill
All rights reserved
Printed in the United States of America
Library of Congress Catalog Card Number: 82-80287

ISBN-10: 0-89750-079-2
ISBN-13: 978-0-89750-079-1

Fifteenth printing 2006

BLACK BELT BOOKS
A Division of **OHARA** 🔟 **PUBLICATIONS, INC.**
World Leader in Martial Arts Publications

THE PEOPLE WHO MADE THIS BOOK

FRANK HILL has been a cartoonist for over 20 years. He is probably best known for his syndicated comic strip, "Short Ribs." Hill has illustrated comic books, advertising, animation, educational books, and design graphics. He became an interested and enthusiastic follower of the martial arts through his son, Troy. Hill and his wife, dancer Carol Mack, have three children: Debbie, Holly, and Troy. They live in Soquel, California.

TED MANCUSO, a writer, has been studying the martial arts for over 14 years. During this time he has taught Karate, Kung Fu, and Tai Chi. While teaching, Mancuso has gained particular enjoyment from instructing young people. He now lives in either Santa Cruz or San Francisco, depending on the season.

Also special thanks to the teachers and students of the Yen Ching school in Santa Cruz, California, for their help with this book.

In China, rice is grown in large submerged fields called paddies. These fields are sometimes hundreds of years old. And yet, every year, a whole new crop comes to them to be harvested, to be eaten, and to nourish the farmer and his family. The martial arts are like this. They are over 4,000 years old. But only when new people learn them and become proficient do they nourish the people and make them strong.

My name is Fu, which means "tiger" in Chinese, and I would like to show you about these ancient arts.

PREFACE (FOR ADULTS)

Like fencing, boxing, archery, and other "martial arts" of the West, Kung Fu has for centuries meant more than mere fighting in China. It improves grace, increases eye/hand coordination, augments flexibility, teaches courage, expresses movement and form, and promotes health.

Neither Kung Fu nor its sister art, Karate, needs equipment or practice partners. Their emphasis on form and technique make them as akin to dance as to boxing. And for young males in some cases, they are the only socially acceptable entrance into the joy of body movement.

When your son, for instance, has been studying for awhile he will begin to see a totally unexpected difference between himself and his schoolmates. He will find that physical movement is much easier to understand—he no longer will have trouble telling his left foot from his right, or dialectical moves from oppositional ones. The progressively structured aspect of his training will make his mind analytical, and as his understanding of his own body increases he will find ease and grace in sports and movements his peers find difficult.

When your daughter takes up the art she will learn to express power as well as grace along with a gained feeling of confidence and self-sufficiency.

After awhile they will begin to find that the historical and cultural aspects of the martial arts are as interesting as the physical. And if they continue their study they will find yet another level—the philosophical and spiritual—which will be the most rewarding of all.

This book was written to teach the basics of that physical level. But it also has the dual purpose of hinting, through story and picture, at the higher levels of Kung Fu and Karate. There is an ancient Chinese adage saying that to perfect Kung Fu one need only "a little proper instruction, a little health, and a strong sense of perseverance." This book will make an expert of no one. The movements it outlines are universal to all major systems of Kung Fu. But with proper study an average young person, helped by a little benign pedagogy from his parent, should be able to attain a strong foundation.

The second purpose of the book is created by the incredible proliferation of Kung Fu and Karate schools in this country. Unfortunately not all schools emphasize the internal aspects of the art as much as the physical. This book is written in such a way that the instructional continuity also explains the relationship of chivalry to Kung Fu. The *Technique* section employs a method in which the strikes and escapes utilize targets that are not vital, that are transferred from the really dangerous zones of the body. The *Games* section has martial arts-related crafts and two-person practice games with a strong accent on helpfulness and partnership. It is hoped that through these subtle but definite implications a young person in an area where personal instruction is unavailable will get a true idea of the spirit of Kung Fu which, in the original Chinese, means, "discipline."

KUNG FU HISTORY

Most of what we know about the history of Kung Fu and Karate comes from legends. Kung Fu seems to be as old as time, because people have always needed to know how to defend themselves against "bad" men and dangerous animals. From early ideas some Chinese monks and nuns developed a system to protect themselves and, at the same time, to make themselves strong so that they would live long and be of great help to the common people. They named the system they invented after the temple in which they lived. The name of the temple was the Young Forest Temple, which in the Chinese language is *Shaolin*. Eventually, this form of self-defense became very famous throughout China and the world. This is what we call Kung Fu.

What would it be like if you lived in these ancient times and wanted to study Kung Fu? Well, first of all you would have to go to a great temple to be accepted as a student. You might have to trudge through a thick, overgrown forest in Northern China for a long while before you came to the huge outer door of the temple. You would knock, and a gnarled old monk with a shaved head would look out.

"What do you want?" he would snarl.

"To be allowed to study in your great temple."

"Go away!" he would say before slamming the door.

Then the waiting would begin. Often a prospective student like you would wait outside a door for at least three days. Eventually, though, you would be allowed to enter the monastery, and then more tests would begin.

In old China a young apprentice would often be given trials for temper or patience. You would be told to cut pieces of meat which the old monks knew were very tough. People would watch and see if you got angry and started hacking at the meat. Even eating would be a test. For the first meal in the temple you might be given a bowl with a hole in the bottom and a large round biscuit. The monk passing out the food would say, "Be sure not to eat the biscuit yet. Have patience." If you ate the biscuit, you would be dismissed from the monastery immediately. If you had patience and waited, you would then be given soup. The proper procedure would be to put the biscuit over the hole in the bowl, let the monk fill the bowl with soup, drink the soup, and then eat the biscuit. This was a test of intelligence as well as patience.

Finally, you would be formally accepted, and if your heart was good you would be taught all the secret and unusual moves of the art of Kung Fu. You would practice many hours a day for a number of years, and from time to time, you would be tested to make sure that your progress was satisfactory. At last, as the legend goes, you would come to the final test conducted in a

Great Hall of Dummies. The Hall was supposed to contain 108 wooden dummies, each mechanically constructed to attack with one distinct movement when someone walked on the floorboards of the Hall. At the end of the Hall there was a door with a great heated stone urn in front of it. If you had made it that far you were required to lift the urn and move it from the door. In the act of moving the urn you would have both your forearms branded by the hot stone with a tiger on one arm and a dragon on the other. These symbols showed that you were a graduate of the Shaolin Temple style of Karate and a master of Kung Fu.

The years passed and Kung Fu spread from the Shaolin Temple until it was being practiced throughout China. People, trying to improve the art, found that they could learn a great deal from watching and imitating animals in their movements. They soon developed Kung Fu styles based on tigers, cranes, snakes, leopards, bears, and various insects. There were even dog, cat, rat, and chicken forms of Kung Fu.

After Kung Fu had been practiced in China for about a thousand years, some people—mostly monks and sailors—took the art to the countries outside of China. One man, shipwrecked in a place called Okinawa, was discovered by the natives and in return for saving his life he taught them a simple version of Kung Fu which they later called *Te,* or "hand." Sometimes, to commemorate where it came from, they called this wonderful fighting art *Kara Te,* or "Chinese hand."

The Okinawans developed Kara Te into an art all their own. They had often had trouble defending their islands against invaders. They practiced their new martial art with a warrior spirit and an emphasis on hard, fast, strong moves. It was a time of war for them, so they simplified the original Chinese art to be as practical as possible.

Some Okinawan masters worked very hard to perfect the new Kara Te. They stood in the Horse stance for hours, punched thousands of times while standing at the bottom of tumbling waterfalls, and they drove themselves to new strengths. Some masters wore their belts, generally white, so long a time that the belts became completely black over the years. This is thought to be where the modern-day black belt rank was born.

From Okinawa the art spread to Japan where it was also called Karate. But this meant "empty hand," not "Chinese hand," in the Japanese language. In Japan it was first practiced as a sport and later as a means of self-defense. After World War II people became aware of this intriguing art, and from Japan it spread throughout the world.

CONTENTS

STRETCHING

You should always warm up for at least ten minutes before you practice. Warming up prepares the muscles for hard activity and shows the proper respect for your body.

When you stretch, though, you are not only stretching the muscles. You are also stretching the arteries. These are like hoses that carry blood throughout the body. As you age, the arteries begin to develop a hard crust inside them; a crust that stretching helps to prevent. If you stretch a lot you can keep yourself limber for a long time.

All stretching is good. Do the ones you have learned from school sports, dance class, whatever. Also, try some of the exercises described in this section.

BUTTERFLIES

For this one you can sit down. Put the bottoms of your feet together in front of you. Then grab your ankles with both hands and pull them in until your feet are almost touching your body. Now all you do is gently bounce your knees. You will feel the stretch in your inner thighs.

This is one of the best exercises for the thighs. You need this kind of limberness to do thrust kicks, as you'll see. Some karate experts are so limber they can kick hats off their own heads (though generally they just take them off).

BEND AND STRETCH

WARMING UP IS IMPORTANT. A JOURNEY OF 1000 MILES BEGINS WITH ONE STEP.

You are probably going to feel this one right behind your knees. The tendons back there are being stretched. This is good for all kicks to the front, all your stances—just about everything.

Bend forward and keep your knees straight. Reach down as far as you can, trying to touch the floor with your fingertips. If this is pretty easy try touching your fists to the floor, then your palms. Gently bounce ten times.

If you are really limber try holding your head to your knees for a count of ten. Again, don't bend your knees.

BODY CIRCLES

When I was young and very lazy, this was my favorite warm-up exercise because it was so easy. I could do it even on cold mornings.

Hip Circles: Place your feet about as far apart as your shoulders. Put your hands on your hips. Now circle your hips ten times in each direction (20 times wouldn't hurt). But don't bend your knees. We are saving them for . . .

Knee Circles: Put your hands on your knees. Now circle them ten times in each direction. When your knees are back your legs should be straight. When they are forward, you should be squatting.

ARM CIRCLES

This exercise loosens the shoulders and improves circulation to the arms. It is another good way to warm up on cold days.

Face right. Then circle your left arm backwards in the biggest circle possible. Spin it just like an airplane propeller or a helicopter blade. Do at least 20 circles. Then face left and repeat with the other arm. When you are through, your hands will be pinkish. Rub them together.

SPINE STRETCH

The spine, the masters say, should be loose as a snake's body.
Your back bone is made of many discs connected like pearls
on a string and held together by muscles. These muscles can
be stretched and kept flexible. Here's one way . . .

Spread your feet
apart and hold
arms out in front
of your chest.

1.

Without moving
your feet or hips,
turn your waist
to the left . . .

2.

Keep rotating until
you are in a back
bend (don't go
over too far at
first—try this on
the lawn just in
case). Keep
turning until . . .

3.

You have come
around on the right
side. Now rotate
that way four more
times. Then rotate
five times in the
other direction.

4.

PUSHING THE MOUNTAIN

This exercise takes a little imagination. Get into a good solid stance with your feet wide apart. Put your hands up as though you were about to push the side of a mountain. Now slowly push the mountain away, using all your power. As you push, breathe out slowly making a sound like the hissing of a snake. This is not only good for the arms and shoulder but it strengthens the legs as well.

FINGER EXERCISES

One good way to strengthen the hands is a push-up on the finger-tips. But take it slow. Five is plenty to begin. Then build from there.

This exercise comes from the ancient Eagle Claw style of Kung Fu. Grab an empty jar with just the tips of your fingers and try to hold it at arm's length for one minute. If that is easy add a little water to the jar and try again. When you can hold a jar full of water that way start adding sand. (Don't use a jar your parents might want, though.)

KUNG FU AND KARATE TRY TO WORK ALL PARTS OF THE BODY: EVEN THE FINGERS.

SINGLE-LEG SQUATS

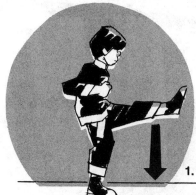

This is one of the hardest and best exercises for leg strength.

Hold your leg straight out. Try not to touch the floor with that front heel.

1.

Squat straight down close to the floor, then lift yourself straight up. If it helps, put your arms out in front of your chest. Keep your back heel close to the ground.

2.

Try not to use your arms except for balance. Don't touch the floor with your hands.

3.

WORK UP TO TEN OF THESE WITH EACH LEG AND YOUR KICKS WILL IMPROVE.

STANCES

The first thing you are going to learn in this section is stance, or how to stand. Stance in the martial arts means how you hold your weight, how protected you are from attack, and at the same time, how ready you are to strike out.

It is really hard at first to get anything done without a stance, even though we don't always think about it. Have you ever noticed how a cat wiggles its rear and digs its claws in before leaping on a toy? How would you feel trying to run a race without starting from a good crouch? Or how about being at the front line in a football game standing up like you're waiting for a bus? When you are in a good stance, you feel like an arrow waiting to explode out of a bow.

But standing correctly isn't enough. You have to move correctly too. So after the *Stance* section we have some words about *Footwork.* Get comfortable with one, then try the other.

THE HORSE

The *Horse* stance is the basic martial arts stance. It strengthens the legs and makes you more stable.

Spread your feet apart a little wider than your shoulders. Make them as parallel as railroad tracks. Then bend your knees down, then out until they are over your feet. Each leg should carry 50 percent of your weight. Keep your back straight.

THE HORSE

There are a lot of different *kinds* of Horse stances. They have different names depending on where your opponent is standing.

If your center line (an imaginary line that runs down the center of your body) is facing your opponent, then this is the *Square Horse.* You only use this portion for exercise.

If you turn one side to the opponent and stand sideways to him or her, this is the *Side Horse.*

Every Side Horse has two legs: the front leg—the one closer to your partner; and the rear leg—the one farther away from your partner. This Side Horse is always named after its front leg. A Side Horse with *right* front leg is called a Right Side Horse.

HIDDEN FOOT STANCE

The *Hidden Foot* is a deceptive stance. The rear foot is held heel up as straight as a telephone pole. The front foot is flat. This is a good step for retreating.

You get into this stance by standing with your feet as far apart as your shoulders, then simply stepping ahead with one foot.

This is a good stance for sudden twisting moves. In this one you pull a person off balance.

CRANE STANCE

The crane is a beautiful white bird much esteemed among the Chinese for its majesty and grace.
The *Crane* stance is one where you lift one leg up in the air with your knees bent and your toes pointed.

Three-way kicks from the Crane stance: Knee. Thrust Kick. Snap Kick. Rear Kick.

Rear Kick

Thrust Kick

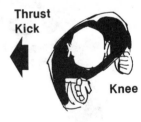

Knee

Snap Kick

The important thing to know about the Crane stance is this: you can't kick without it. Every time you raise your leg, you go through this stance. Therefore you should learn to be comfortable in the Crane stance. Stand in it for a count of ten then hop onto the other leg. Then hop back and try to kick.

THE CAT STANCE

The *Cat* stance is a graceful stance. It allows lightning-fast kicks from the front foot.

To enter a Left Cat, step back with your right foot so your right toe points to a corner. Now bend that right knee and lower your rear end as if you were sitting in a chair. Keep your back straight.

Now, raise your left (front) heel so that just the ball of that foot rests lightly on the ground. If you weigh 100 pounds, only five of them should be on your front foot.

NOW FOR AN EVEN BIGGER CAT...

RIDE THE TIGER STANCE

Stand with your feet wide apart. Then, lower your weight onto one leg. Try to keep both heels flat on the ground. One hand guards the face, the other guards the ribs.

Ride the Tiger stance was developed to drop suddenly under high kicks. It is also an excellent exercise for the inner thigh, if you go slowly at first.

SEVEN STAR STANCE

The *Seven Star* stance is a lot like the Cat stance. It is also a lot like just walking around. This time your back leg is bent, but your heel touches the ground.

This stance can be used as a kind of step on your opponent's front leg.

Bend the back knee.

It stops kicks—fast!

The front heel only touches the ground lightly, as though it were resting on a matchbox.

If you could not do the Single Leg Squats on page 19, try them in this stance. Let your front heel lightly slide along the floor as you go up and down.

THE GROUND STANCE

There are two main reasons for the *Ground* stance. 1) It helps us to do something better, like a Crane stance helps us to kick; 2) It protects us by making it harder to hit us. Protecting yourself means getting into a position where your body is harder to hit, and you can strike back. One time you really need a stance is when you fall down . . .

Front view

Points to remember:

Front leg up, knee aimed at opponent.

Kick to front leg.

Front hand up to cover face.

Curl your back foot under so it cannot be stomped.

Stretch out your back hand for balance.

POSITIONING THE ARMS

One hand span

One fist span

Stances aren't just the position of the legs. The arms guard the upper body and, if they are not in their proper position, there are all sorts of "tunnels" and openings for the opponent to strike through. This is just about the perfect positon for a beginner to start with.

Shoulder high

FOOTWORK

Stances are positions. They help to protect you, but they are useless without footwork, like a car is without gas.

This section tells you about moving. A good martial artist moves like water. First learn the three basic moves: step, shuffle, replacement. Then mix them up every way you can think of.

Remember: Don't just go back and forth like a trolley car. Learn to move in all directions.

THE ROOF

In the martial arts there is something called *The Roof Law.* This means that whenever you move, you act as though the roof in your house had been lowered until it was about two inches above your head. Now, don't touch that roof! Whether you are stepping, kicking, or punching try not to bob up and touch your new roof.

A few words about footwork. Karate people use special terms for different kinds of foot movements. There are three basic words you should know to study self-defense.

The Step: There is only one true *step* in Karate. This happens when your back foot passes all the way through and becomes your front foot. Just like when you walk. These next two movements are sometimes called steps but not in the martial arts . . .

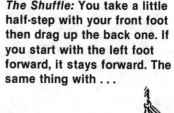

The Shuffle: You take a little half-step with your front foot then drag up the back one. If you start with the left foot forward, it stays forward. The same thing with . . .

The Replacement: In this you move your back foot first and then step out with your front foot. Try all these steps, forward and back, with kicks and hand moves. Try to be smooth and quick.

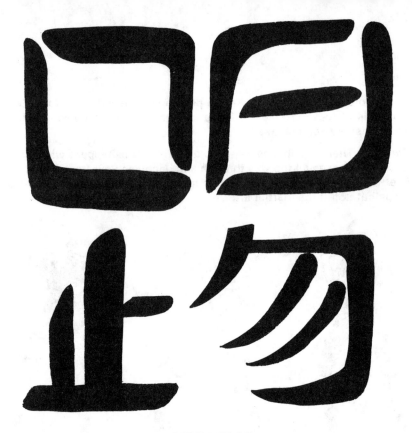

KICKING

Kicks are very effective. But they require a good deal of skill to do well. The leg is a powerful weapon. It has three obvious advantages:

1. It is longer than the arm. A four-foot six-inch person has a leg that is longer than the arm of a six-foot person.
2. The legs are four to five times as strong as the arms.
3. The legs hit from underneath and other hard-to-block angles.

However, there are some *disadvantages* too:

1. You are not as balanced on one leg as two. (This means you have to kick *fast*, before someone grabs your leg.)
2. Most people are not as comfortable kicking as hitting. (That means that good kicking takes three things: practice, practice, and practice. And that's what this section is all about.)

FRONT SNAP KICK

This is probably the basic kick of the martial arts. But doing it right takes practice.

From a Left Horse stance . . .

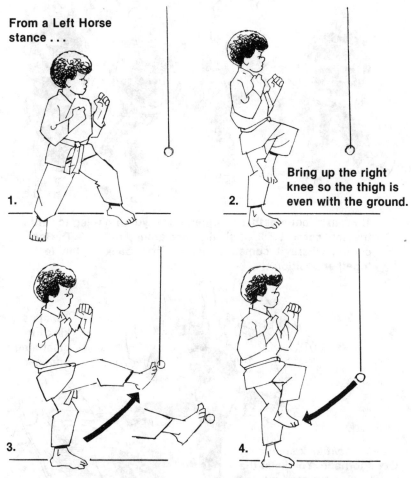

1.

2. Bring up the right knee so the thigh is even with the ground.

3. Curl the toes back. Kick out with the ball of the foot, but don't move the knee an inch!

4. Bring it back along the same path. Your knee still shouldn't move. Then replace your foot.

The knee should be kept "frozen." Moving the knee in this kick is like jerking your elbow just as you shoot an arrow. Also, try this kick off the front foot from a Cat stance.

CRESCENT KICK

1. From a feet-together position, throw your right leg toward the right corner . . . 2. Circle it up and around to . . . 3. The left corner, where it comes down. 4. Then back to the feet-together position.

This is a good kick for disarming an opponent.

The *Crescent* kick should hit like a tornado. You keep the kicking leg straight and swing it in a high arc from one side to another. At the high point of the kick you can slap your opposite hand.

This kick is named after the Crescent Moon.

THE REAR KICK

You are walking down a dark, windy street. There is a noise behind you. You glance over your shoulder to see a dark, huge shape looming over you. There is no time to turn around. What do you do? Answer: *Rear* kick.

1. Bend over so your chest is even with the ground (and your head is away from your opponent). Cock your kicking leg. Glance back over your shoulder.

2.

Shoot your heel out as straight as an arrow.

3.

Once the kick is done, pull that leg back as fast as you can so you can kick again if you need to. (You are also in a perfect position to run away, which is always a good move.)

THE THRUST KICK

1.

Thrusting (going straight) and Swinging (going around) are the two main types of movement in everything including Karate, Judo, Aikido, Kung Fu, and the rest.
The Thrust kick not only goes straight but is one of the most powerful kicks you can throw.

2.

From a Left Horse stance . . .

Cock your left knee so it is pointing straight out in front of your body, not at the target. (The Crane stance, remember?)

3.

Then push with the
knee to thrust the
heel straight at the
opponent.

Keep your arms
there. Don't flap them
like bird wings.
Bend a little for
balance.
Let the standing foot
turn away from the
kick if that is more
comfortable.

Stand with your back to a wall
to practice. If you do the kick
perfectly straight, you won't
touch the wall.

THE WHEEL KICK

The *Wheel* kick is one of the quickest, easiest, and best kicks. Here is a good way to start:

1.

You are in a Left Horse. Imagine an empty table in front of you about waist high.

2.

Bring your left leg straight up so your knee, shin, and foot are atop this table. This is important. It is known as the *Wheel Cock* position. Just try that a few times.

From above: Your foot raises toward the back so it is right behind your knee.

3.

From the last position, quickly snap the kick out and back. Strike with the ball of the foot. Then, of course, you can put your foot down.

At its final position, the Wheel looks like the Thrust but it is *completely* different. A Thrust goes straight. The Wheel swings.

Thrust Kick

Wheel Kick

LOOK THROUGH THE WHOLE *KICKS* SECTION. WHAT KICK IS THE WHEEL MOST LIKE? SAME ACTION, DIFFERENT ANGLE.

IF YOU SAID "*SNAP KICK*" YOU ARE RIGHT. A WHEEL IS A SNAP TURNED SIDEWAYS.

JUMP — SNAP

Some styles specialize in jumping and leaping so much that the people who do them are known as *Flyers.* Almost any kick you can do on the ground you can do in the air, if you are good enough. Here is a simple one.

3.

Snap kick when you are at your highest. Important: pull that leg back before you touch the ground.

2.

Leap into the air, tucking up your kicking leg knee.

Start low—a good Flying kick is the same whether it is six inches or six feet off the ground. Perfect your form before your height.

1.

From the feet-together position ... Squat down until your fingers can touch the ground. Then ...

THE JART

The *Jart* is a special kick. It comes from Southern China and Okinawa. It is very good for short range kicking.

From a Left Horse stance . . .

1.

Then stomp downward with the arch of your foot. Right after that withdraw your leg back to Step One as fast as you can.

2.

Raise your right knee straight up, as though pointing out from your stomach. Here's the Crane stance again.

This is an especially good kick to stop other kicks.

THE MONKEY SCISSORS KICK

Monkeys live all through Southeast Asia. They are extremely intelligent and gentle, but they can also be very crafty. For instance, this kick from a style of Kung Fu called the *Iron Monkey* style . . .

You can do this kick if you are lying on the ground or if you fall to the ground to surprise an opponent. If your left leg is on the bottom, stretch it out. Cock your right knee way up to your chest.

Then *push* out with your right foot as you *pull* back with your left. Keep your left ankle bent; that's a Hook.

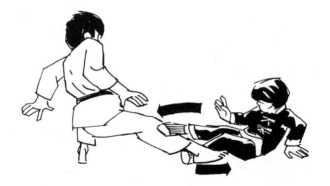

You generally do this kick against a front leg to force the opponent to the ground.

STOP KICK

The *Stop* kick is almost more of a leg lift than a kick. All you do is raise your front foot about eight inches off the ground and use the edge of it to block an opponent's kick or rush.

The Stop kick is one of the fastest and most effective kicks there is. This is especially true if you don't know what your opponent has in mind. It is rather like a jab with the foot.

THE SWEEP

Sweeping is used to knock an opponent down. If you can grab at the same time and tug down, you will make everything happen even faster.

There are a few good things to know about sweeps. If you know what a lever is, you know that the farther out you push on a lever, the more you can lift.

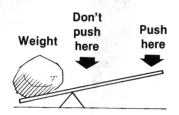

A person's leg is like a lever. The more toward the end (the ankle) you sweep it, the more *push* you will have.

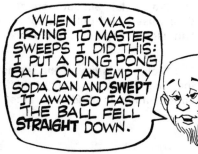

WHEN I WAS TRYING TO MASTER SWEEPS I DID THIS: I PUT A PING PONG BALL ON AN EMPTY SODA CAN AND **SWEPT** IT AWAY SO FAST THE BALL FELL **STRAIGHT** DOWN.

TURN AROUND
MULE KICK

1. This is a kick that goes around behind you. If you start with your right leg back ...

Turn to the right. Put both hands on the ground. Bring up your right heel ...

2.

3. Look over your right shoulder as you thrust your right heel out.

Put your right foot down toward your opponent.

4.

You should be good at this kick even when you are playing. This is advanced, so perfect the others first. Don't put the cart before the mule.

DOUBLE KICK

When you do more than one kick before putting your foot down this is called a *Combination* kick. Combination kicks are a great way to practice balance.

Once you feel comfortable with your Snap and Rear kicks, try this *Double* kick.

3.
Then cock
your leg back.

Do a front Snap
kick with your
2. right leg.

Cock your
1. knee and ...

Bend over and bring your shin level with the floor.

5.

Look over your right shoulder. Thrust back with your right Rear kick.

Then cock your leg back in case you want to kick again. If you find yourself falling forward, try to pull your Rear kick back a little shorter. Do the same thing if you find that your Rear kick is hooking upward at the knee.

6.

Pick two spots on the wall (but don't really kick them) in front and behind you, and see if you can kick at them in less than three seconds.

SNAP KICK –WHEEL KICK

This is an excellent combination for speed. Practice it off both sides until it is absolutely natural.

1.

Cock your left leg and throw a Snap kick . . .

2.

After bringing your left foot back, lift your heel so that you are in the Wheel Cock position. Don't put your foot down.

3.

Cock your right knee high . . .

4.

Now snap out the wheel kick. Then replace your foot.

The way to use the Snap Wheel: Half the time you don't even need to complete the first kick. Just raise your knee, and when your sparring partner drops his or her hand to block the Snap Kick, go around with a Wheel.

Use these combinations, and make up your own. Practice kicking at least twice before putting your foot down.

THE MANY FACES OF THE MARTIAL ARTS

There are probably more than a thousand styles of martial arts. For hundreds of years people have developed and improved on the older arts not only for fighting skill but for grace, health, and just for fun. Here are some of those major arts.

KARATE: The art of the "empty hand." Karate is mostly striking and kicking. Originally Kung Fu was wrestling (Jujitsu) and striking (Karate). After it left China and went to Okinawa, it split into two branches, and the hitting part became known as Karate. There are many styles of Karate but all of it is based on explosive power and speedy execution.

KUNG FU: This is the oldest martial art. It dates back over 4,000 years. In old China, it was considered one of the five arts for an educated person to master. The other four included medicine, painting, poetry, and calligraphy (brush writing). Generally, Kung Fu is very circular and fast.

JUDO: Or the "gentle way." This sport, based on Jujitsu, uses trips, throws, locks, and chokes. Because it is a sport, it can have contests without people getting hurt. Sparring in Judo is called *"Randori,"* and it is one method of gaining higher rank.

AIKIDO: Is a Japanese art. It was developed in this century. Most Aikido moves try not to damage the opponent too much. Aikido students like to spin, toss, and throw their opponents. It is a particularly beautiful art to watch.

Thai Boxing: Thailand is another Oriental nation. Here the art form is a combination of Eastern kicking and Western boxing (introduced by the French). Thai Boxing matches are exciting, fast paced, and very famous throughout the martial arts world.

Sumo: Sumo is a favorite spectator sport in Japan. Matches are often very short and only last about 15 seconds. And since one of the objects is to push the other wrestler out of the circle inscribed on the floor, it helps to be a very heavy person in this art!

Kendo: Japanese fencing. Kendo is a fast paced form with a lot of sparring. Real swords have been replaced by bamboo ones and body armor protects the students from the machine gun-fast blows of their opponents.

Kenpo: Actually, Kenpo is a Japanese word for Kung Fu. However, over the years, Kenpo has become a separate style of movement that puts together extremely fast hand moves and modern principles of science. It is very popular in Hawaii and continental America.

Tae Kwon Do: This is a newer version of Korean Karate. In the old days it was called *Kwon Bop.* TKD is about 80 percent kicks and 20 percent hands. Craftsmen in ancient Korea did not want to damage their hands in combat so they developed this wonderful kicking art.

THE HANDS

Hand fighting in Karate and Kung Fu is different from boxing. In boxing the hands are held in one position—a fist. In Karate they may have to change shape to do different things (see the *Blocking* section on page 68). This is known as specialization; that is, a special hand for a special job. Also, some positions are just plain fun. They were invented hundreds of years ago and represent various ideas—animals, birds, or tools. All hand positions are really just that—Tools. Early people might have looked at the way a knife cuts and tried to imitate it. They came up with the chop. They also created the *Spear* hand. the *Hammerfist,* and the *Yoke* hand in the same manner. They looked out windows and saw animals using their paws, claws, talons, feelers and tails. What would it feel like, they wondered, to have a paw like a bear? Or a cat? Or a claw like an eagle? Thus, as always, imagination preceded everything.

THE LEOPARD FIST

Leopards are spotted cats. They are smart, strong, and *very* fast. Leopards run at speeds over 60 miles an hour.

The *Leopard* fist is a quick, short movement. Because it is formed by folding the fingers halfway down, it is also known as the *Half* fist.

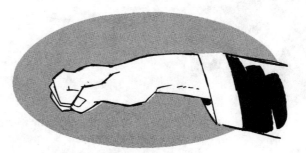

When you form the Leopard fist remember to tightly fold the pads of your fingertips toward your palm. Also make sure your thumb is tucked in; don't have it sticking out like a car antenna.

THE RAM'S HEAD FIST

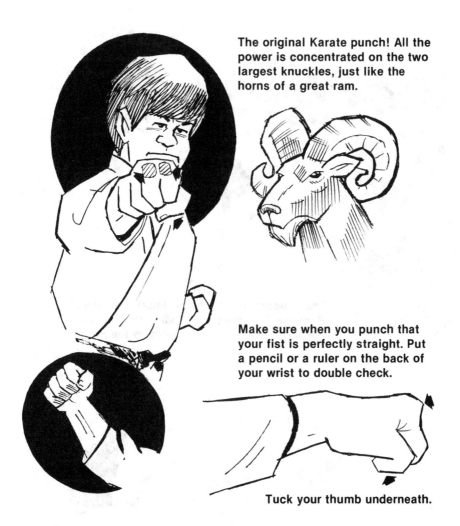

The original Karate punch! All the power is concentrated on the two largest knuckles, just like the horns of a great ram.

Make sure when you punch that your fist is perfectly straight. Put a pencil or a ruler on the back of your wrist to double check.

Tuck your thumb underneath.

The *Ram's Head* fist is so powerful because the force is so concentrated. Let's say you weigh 100 pounds. If you hit with the flat of your fist, that's 20 pounds per inch (100 divided by 5). *But* if you hit with just the two knuckles, let's say one inch, that's *100 pounds per inch*. Quite a difference!

It is not enough to know how to hold a fist, though. You have to know how to punch. You will find that this method of thrusting works with just about all the other hand forms in this section.

The punch starts with the fist cocked at the side, palm up.

When the punch is halfway out, the palm is half turned over.

All the way out the punch is turned over with a snap, palm down. The elbow is bent very slightly. Keep your shoulder relaxed. If you tense up it is like putting a kink in a hose; it will stop up the power.

While all this is going on, the other arm is pulling back to the cocked position with just as much force, like your legs do when they are pumping a bicycle.

THE BACK KNUCKLE

The *Back Knuckle* or *Back Fist* is a swinging motion from the elbow. It is sort of a Snap kick with the arm. The elbow is frozen in space, then the lower arm whips out and back.

When you strike with this you can hit with the whole hand or just the backs of the two big knuckles.

1.

All you do is raise your elbow and point it, snap your Back fist out, then draw it back in.

2.

3.

The Back knuckle is one of the fastest motions. Try whipping it out with the same movement you would use to snap a towel. Make your move brisk. Don't raise your shoulder. Try it with a shuffle (see the *Footwork* section on page 30).

CRANE HAND

Besides standing over five feet tall and being able to spread its wings longer than eight feet, the crane has a long, slender beak. When angered it flaps its huge wings and pecks out fiercely.

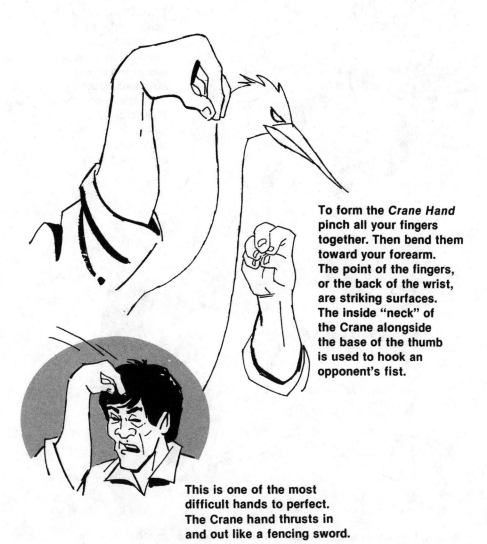

To form the *Crane Hand* pinch all your fingers together. Then bend them toward your forearm. The point of the fingers, or the back of the wrist, are striking surfaces. The inside "neck" of the Crane alongside the base of the thumb is used to hook an opponent's fist.

This is one of the most difficult hands to perfect. The Crane hand thrusts in and out like a fencing sword.

TIGER CLAW

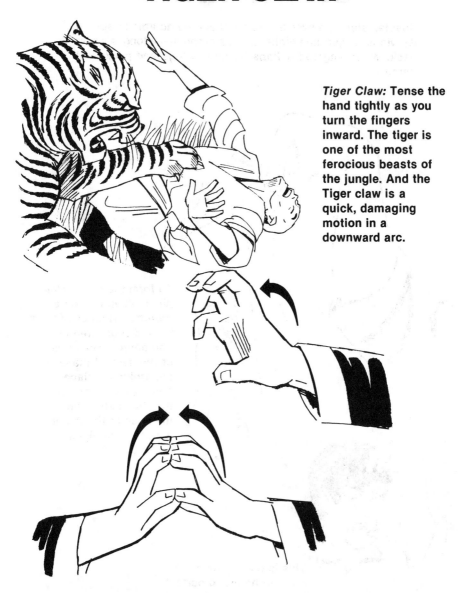

Tiger Claw: Tense the hand tightly as you turn the fingers inward. The tiger is one of the most ferocious beasts of the jungle. And the Tiger claw is a quick, damaging motion in a downward arc.

To strengthen the claw, press your fingers together as hard as you can for a count of ten.

WHITE SNAKE HAND

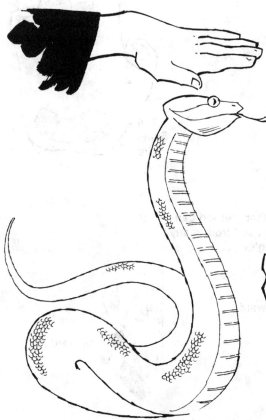

Long ago, in ancient China, Kung Fu was divided into two arts—*Iron hand* and *Poison hand.* Iron hand techniques were modeled after making the limbs just like weapons; the fist into a mace, the legs into iron poles. People would hit bricks, trees and iron pellets to condition themselves. Poison hand training modeled itself after animals with speed, like the snake that strikes at 100 miles per hour.

The main things with *Snake Hand* training are speed and accuracy. The tips of the fingers are used to jab and sting like the fangs of a snake. A hanging ball (see the *Games* section on page 86) is one of the best ways to train this weapon.

LARGE AND SMALL STARS

The palm is an amazing part of the hand. It is soft yet very strong. In the martial arts it is used in two ways:

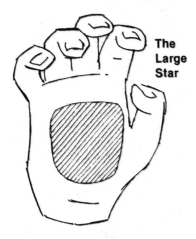

The Large Star

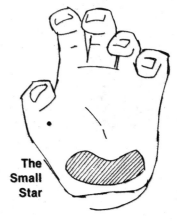

The Small Star

Either method can be used from many angles . . .

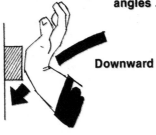

Downward

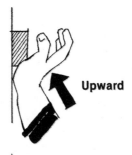

Upward

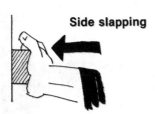

Side slapping

Straight

WILLOW LEAF PALM

The *Willow Leaf Palm* is basically the same thing as the Karate chop you see in the movies or on TV. It comes in two versions, though—straight and bent.

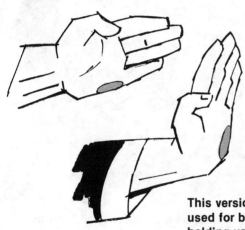

The straight form is used for cutting motions. *Make sure your thumb is tucked down so it doesn't catch on anything.* Also, curl your fingers a bit to tense the hand.

This version with the wrist bent is used for blocking and exercise. Just holding your hand like this can strengthen your wrist and forearm.

Two bent willow leaves crossed form a *Scissor Hand Block.*

DRAGON HANDS

Dragons are mythical (imaginary) creatures. They have bodies as long as school yards, skin rougher than tree bark, and they float through the sky like clouds. In the Orient they are considered to be good natured. They live in wells and bring rain to farmers. These hand positions represent different parts of those beautiful beasts.

Dragon Claw: Spread all five fingers apart from one another. Then bend and tighten the tips of your fingers just a little. Feel the strength. The dragon claw is used in slapping and back slapping motions.

Dragon's Head Fist: Make a fist. Then pop out the middle knuckle. Use the thumb to brace the extended knuckle. The Dragon's Head attacks hard, bony surfaces.

THE EYE OF THE PHOENIX

This is where the *Phoenix Eye* fist got its name.

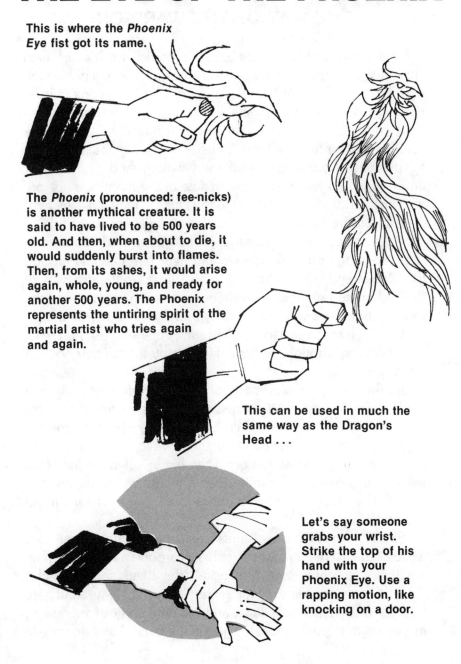

The *Phoenix* (pronounced: fee-nicks) is another mythical creature. It is said to have lived to be 500 years old. And then, when about to die, it would suddenly burst into flames. Then, from its ashes, it would arise again, whole, young, and ready for another 500 years. The Phoenix represents the untiring spirit of the martial artist who tries again and again.

This can be used in much the same way as the Dragon's Head . . .

Let's say someone grabs your wrist. Strike the top of his hand with your Phoenix Eye. Use a rapping motion, like knocking on a door.

THE WAY OF THE WARRIOR

Here is a very old story all about the martial arts. Yet, its main character is a cook. This man was the head cook of a noble Chinese lord, the Duke of Chou. This particular head cook, whose name no one quite remembers, was a strange character. He was fiesty and fat and yelled out loud, then mumbled to himself as he cut the meat for the day's meal. Half the time he would show up sleepy-eyed, scratching himself and yawning, and then at other times he would wake up in the middle of the night, long before the birds had started to sing, go to the Duke's huge, cold kitchen, start up all the fires, chop up all the ingredients, and begin to cook up some new delicacy that had come to him in a dream.

Some of the other servants could hear him banging around the kitchen and talking aloud. They would go to the doorway of the kitchen and see the weird shadows dancing on the walls, the roasting meat wet with melting fat, and the cook madly mixing sauces like a sorcerer. No one had the courage to ask him what he was doing, though, or why. He was by far the best cook in the castle.

But the thing the head cook did the absolute best was meat cutting. Even though all the assistant cooks watched him cut meat all day long, no one could figure out how he did it so easily. The best of the other cooks would have to hack and pound, then throw the meat slab around the big wooden cutting block like a man wrestling a buffalo. Sweat would break out on their brows. They would say fierce things to the meat, like it was an opponent.

Finally, one of the assistants could bear it no longer. So, while all the kitchen help were gathered around a huge wok having their afternoon meal, he asked the head cook outright: "Hey. Come on, tell us your secret." he said. "My hands are blistered from handling a knife, and I sit here and watch you sing as you seem to peel the meat right off the bone. How do you do it? Why is it so easy for you?"

The head cook laughed. "It's very simple," he said picking up his knife to demonstrate in the air on an imaginary flank. "No disrespect to the other cooks here," he bowed. "But while some cooks like to hack, and others prefer to tear, and still another crowd wants to saw," he demonstrated each of these methods, "I cut. I slide my knife into the secret spaces between bone and meat, and *whizz-zip*, separate everything neatly. I follow the bone and the grain of the meat. I never resist the way the meat wants to go. That's why," he said, holding up his knife so they could see it gleam in the light of the spit fire, "cutting with my method actually sharpens my knife. Where other cooks go through four or five knives a year, I have had this one for 12 years now. And it is sharper than the day I got it."

After that the assistants stopped watching the head cook so much, and they started paying more attention to what they were cutting.

This has been a favorite story of martial artists for over a thousand years. Kung Fu and Karate people admire the head cook because he is so original. He never tries to force things unnaturally. One of the main lessons of the martial arts is, "Don't resist." If you meet someone who weighs 300 pounds and he starts to strike at you, you cannot resist. But even if he comes charging at you, leap out of the way and give him a little extra shove so that he will be running away with 310 pounds. You used his strength against him, all without meeting force with force.

A martial artist is always on guard. Everything in life demands a warrior's attitude. Hopefully, you will never need to defend yourself against an attack. But there are conflicts in everyday life. Sometimes when you feel as though you would like to hack, pound, or saw, think about the Duke of Chou's cook and see if there is not an easier way to do what you are doing.

This is the true warrior's way.

BLOCKING ZONES

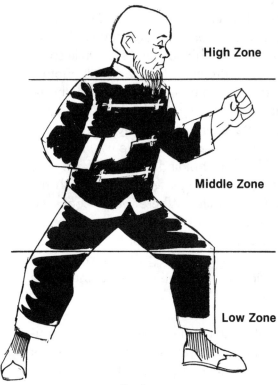

High Zone

Middle Zone

Low Zone

Blocking is entirely devoted to protecting you from attacks. The best block though is simply to move (see the *Footwork* section on page 30). But sometimes you can't dodge a punch. Sometimes you have to use blocks.

To block well you don't worry so much about *what* your opponent is throwing, but *where* it is going. As in basketball you block zones. Think of your body as having three zones of height . . .

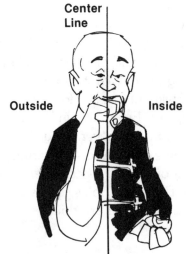

Center Line

Outside

Inside

. . . and two have to do with width. The *Inside* is everything inside your arms. The *Outside* is outside one arm, around your back, to the outside of the other arm.

HIGH AND LOW

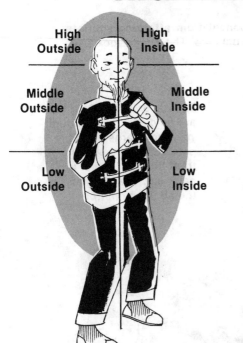

High Outside

High Inside

Middle Outside

Middle Inside

Low Outside

Low Inside

That means there are 2 x 3 zones to cover. That's six.

That's a lot of area to cover! But let's forget about the lowest two for a second and just try to guard the top four.

Since your arms can't be everywhere at once, it is a good idea to use the *High-Low Rule.* That is, if one hand blocks high the other hand immediately drops low *even if there are no visible attacks down there.*

High block for punch, but other hand low to guard stomach

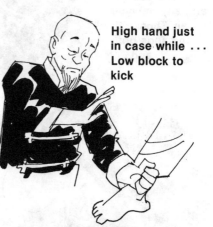

High hand just in case while . . . Low block to kick

The same is true of your opponent. In sparring the idea is to make *his* hands run all over the place. If you attack high with a punch, you should attack low with a kick, or low and then high.

THE DRAG BLOCK

Another way to stop an opponent from attacking you is a method that throws him off balance. The *Drag Block* uses strength against itself.

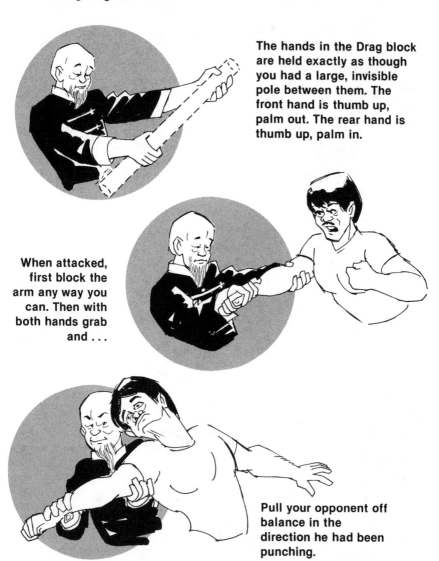

The hands in the Drag block are held exactly as though you had a large, invisible pole between them. The front hand is thumb up, palm out. The rear hand is thumb up, palm in.

When attacked, first block the arm any way you can. Then with both hands grab and . . .

Pull your opponent off balance in the direction he had been punching.

FOLLOWING

No matter how well you block, you cannot stop everything that comes your way. You need a method to counterattack most effectively. One of the best times to do this is just after one of your opponent's attacks. This is called *Following*.

Your opponent attacks.

You block. He begins to draw one hand back so he can hit you with the other.

You follow his retreating punch into him.

BLOCKING EXERCISE

This is a good freestyle exercise for blocking. You must make sure you are very careful though.

A (the person practicing blocks) and B stand in Square Horses facing one another. B puts out both hands. This is to judge distance. B's hands should be at least six inches away from A's chest.

If you are blocking, be sure to keep all your fingers together in a fist. An injured hand is rather unpleasant.

Now, without leaning in, B throws a slow-to-medium-speed punch. A may use any block he wants to. Once A has blocked, B may throw another.

KUMITE

No book can show you everything, but in these next few pages we would like to give you a brief glimpse into other aspects of the martial arts. What you learn from this book will be the foundation for all these advanced studies.

Kumite (koo-mee-tay) is sparring. Two students or experts spar together just as boxers do, but with one difference—they *don't* hit each other. The real skill in Kumite is to execute a powerful, effective blow without striking your opponent. Rather, you *pull* your blow about half an inch before contact.

KATA

A *Kata* (kah-tah) is a "moving book." Long ago, before printing, a martial artist might record everything he or she knew in
a long sequence of moves. These moves looked a little like a
dance that you did alone. People felt that this was the best
way to learn because it made you not only practice the moves
but also the graceful act of getting from one move to another
without stopping. Sometimes a whole series, or form, would
imitate one animal, as in the *Black Tiger* form. You can make
up your own katas by picking a series of moves and making
them flow into one another logically and gracefully. This is a
kind of martial arts shadow boxing.

TAMESHIWARA

Tameshiwara (tommy-shee-war-ah) is the art of breaking bricks, stones, boards and other hard materials (*not* furniture and lamps however!). Through this art we understand the incredible force the body can generate. It is *essential* to have an instructor to teach you this art. Also, many Kung Fu styles don't even use it. They ask, "How many times are you going to be attacked by bricks?"

防御

SELF-DEFENSE

Let's hope you never have to defend yourself. If you are a smart martial artist, you may never have to. Should you need to, however, here are some techniques. Like anything, they take skill. Practicing them will help you to understand the art of "putting things together." It is a lot like music. Kicks, hits, blocks— these are the individual notes. To play music well you must be able to "put it all together." That's really what this section is all about. Either just practicing or suddenly finding that you really *need* a self-defense technique, you may forget what you read here (you probably will). But, if you can go through these techniques without jerking and stopping, the chances are you will be able to move smoothly, no matter what. Probably you are going to practice with a friend. Your friend is not a real opponent trying to hurt you. Not only will he or she *not* react like a real opponent, but he or she should not be treated that way. In other words, don't hit. Be gentle, be patient with one another.

HEADLOCK

Someone has grabbed your neck in a headlock. He has used his right arm.

1.

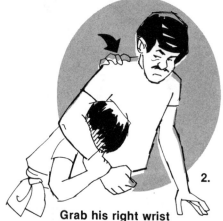

Grab his right wrist with your right hand. At the same time place your left hand behind his right shoulder.

2.

Put your foot behind his right knee. (See *Jart* kick on page 41.)

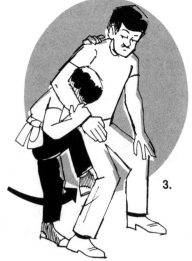

3.

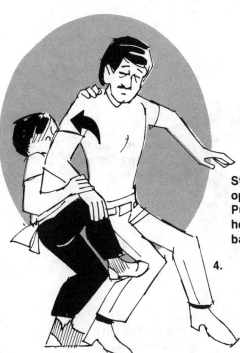

Stomp down behind your
opponent's knee (the Jart).
Pull his wrist and slip your
head out as he loses his
balance.

4.

Force his knee to the
ground. At the same time
stretch his arm back to
keep him helpless.

5.

BEAR HUG
FROM THE FRONT

An attacker has come up from the front and thrown a bear hug on you.

1.

With your free left hand reach back up from behind your opponent and grab the front of his hair. Pull back.

2.

When his jaw starts to go back, put your palm on it and push. Don't worry about the hold. He will let go when he feels himself falling.

3.

BEAR HUG
FROM BEHIND

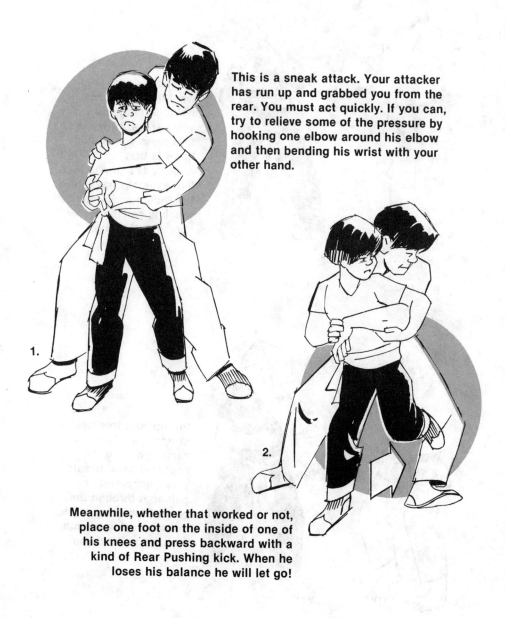

This is a sneak attack. Your attacker has run up and grabbed you from the rear. You must act quickly. If you can, try to relieve some of the pressure by hooking one elbow around his elbow and then bending his wrist with your other hand.

1.

2.

Meanwhile, whether that worked or not, place one foot on the inside of one of his knees and press backward with a kind of Rear Pushing kick. When he loses his balance he will let go!

WRIST GRAB

1.

Someone grabs your wrist. Perhaps he is trying to drag you somewhere. Now the first thing you should know is that somebody's grip is just like a metal ring. Where the thumb and fingers touch is called the "break in the ring."

2.

Put up your free hand to protect your face. At the same time *pull* the captured hand toward you. Concentrate on pulling it through the break in the ring. If you do this briskly enough, no one can hold you.

Pull your free hand to the
cocked position. *Now* you
can stop the technique
there. It is always better to
stop a fight before it starts.
Or, if the opponent tries to
come after you . . .

3.

You can strike him in his chest with your Back fist or Ram's
Head fist. If you are farther away you can use a Thrust or
Snap kick.

WRAP AROUND

This is a good technique because you do not need to hurt your opponent to control him.

Someone comes up and grabs your left shoulder from the side or behind . . .

Pin his fingers with your right hand. ("Pin" means to press something tightly to your body.) Circle your left arm to the front then up and around just like you are painting a huge letter "O."

If you circle all the way around, you will put leverage on your opponent's arm and shoulder. If you wish, you may now remove your right pinning hand and protect yourself with it.

Should he try to strike at you with his free hand, even now, you can "pop" him in the ribs with your left back knuckle.

GAMES AND TOOLS

Games. By "games" in this section we do not mean activities like checkers. Games are simply ways of practicing without repeating a move over and over. True, at first there is no better way to develop skill with a kick than simply kicking over and over. But the time comes when you want to try and test the kick for speed, accuracy, and timing. Kicking or hitting into the air can never quite give you that feeling. You may practice your forearm smash a thousand times in your room but you have to play tennis to really understand how it works. That's what games are for. Remember, though, these are martial arts games. That means, as in any contact sport, there is a bit of a risk involved. *Be careful* with your partner. Practicing with someone is like an electric circuit. When one persons hurts the other, the circuit is broken. Then no one improves.

THE MONGOLIAN DART

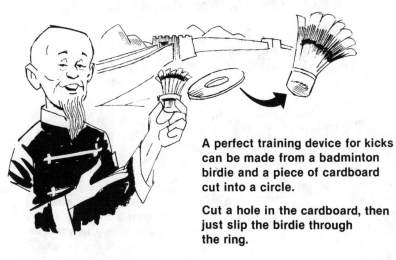

A perfect training device for kicks can be made from a badminton birdie and a piece of cardboard cut into a circle.

Cut a hole in the cardboard, then just slip the birdie through the ring.

Now try to keep this dart airborne (up in the air) as long as possible. Count the number of times you can do this before it hits the ground. Gather some friends in a circle and pass the dart from one to another. You may use your feet, knees, hips, elbows, shoulders, or head, but not your hands.

HIGH FLYING KICK BALL

This is a simple tool, and it is excellent for perfecting accurate kicks.

You will need a tennis ball, a lot of string, and possibly a hook screw or a pulley.

Secure the tennis ball with the string.

Now loop the string over a beam, or the hook, or a tree branch. Then tie the excess string to something. In this way you can raise or lower the ball.

Now the ball is a small moving target. Use every kick you've learned on it. Invent new ones. As you become more limber, move the ball higher. If you have the space, hang more tennis balls up to create "multiple attacks."

TAI CHI SPARRING

Tai Chi (pronounced tie-chee) is a very ancient martial art. It is practiced very slowly. If you wake up in the morning in China and go out to the parks, you can see people of all ages going slowly through their moves. It looks like seaweed floating gently on waves. It is thought that if you practice something slowly, you learn it perfectly. You can use this idea in your practice.

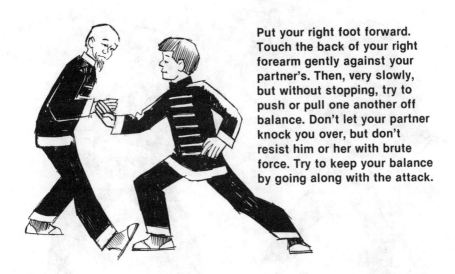

Put your right foot forward. Touch the back of your right forearm gently against your partner's. Then, very slowly, but without stopping, try to push or pull one another off balance. Don't let your partner knock you over, but don't resist him or her with brute force. Try to keep your balance by going along with the attack.

If you learn to play with a lot of slowness and sensitivity, you can even practice as masters do, blindfolded.

STAFF FIGHTING

For this exercise you need a staff. You should be able to get a dowel (rhymes with "towel") from a hardware store. Get one about five feet long.

You and your partner put the same leg forward, let's say left to left. Each of you grabs the staff with your front hand palm up and rear hand palm down.

Now, using just the strength of your legs, and *without* jerking, try to upset one another. Use controlled, smooth strength.

REACTION TELEVISION

Sometimes you can learn something from TV. In this case you may help to speed up your reactions. Put your TV on, but turn off the sound. You may want to lower the lights in your room too. Then get ready. It won't matter what move you do but the instant the picture on the TV changes—*React!* as fast and as hard as you can.

A hint: While waiting for the TV to change, try not to second guess it. Keep your mind as clear as possible.

HANGING PAPER SHIELD

In the very old days in China, martial arts were divided into *Poison Hand* and *Iron Hand* styles. The Iron Hand styles developed tremendous power. This is where the art of board and brick breaking started.

The Poisoned Hand styles were known for their blinding speed. Instead of striking hard things, they trained against soft items like paper, branches, and water.

You can easily make a Poison Hand training device that is very simple. Just hang up a piece of paper (start with something thin like rice paper or thin typing paper) using two strings.

Now comes the hard part: Try to thrust through the paper with your fingertips. Remember the Karate law: If it goes out at 100 miles an hour, it comes back at 125! This snapping back motion increases the sting of each blow.

RAMP AND BALL

THIS IS A TOOL FOR DEVELOPING YOUR LOW KICKS IT IS SIMPLE TO MAKE AND YOU CAN PUT IT UP ANYWHERE.

SAND

Take a medium sized hard rubber ball. Cut a small hole in it.
Fill it with sand and tape the hole securely.

Set up a low ramp against a wall or on any stable surface. As the ball rolls down, strike it back up the ramp with a Stop Kick or any other low strike. If you need to, attach rails to the ramp to keep the ball on track.

FOCUS PAD

An old catcher's mitt can serve as an excellent martial arts focus pad.

Have your practice partner hold it high. The second he sees you move he drops the glove. Try to hit it before it drops.

Move it slowly up and down and have him try to thrust kick this "moving target."

PICKING A SCHOOL

The best way to find a good school is to talk to people. Most instructors are happy to describe what they teach and how they go about it. Many schools will allow spectators. Go in or call up and find out if and when visitors are allowed.

When talking to a head instructor or manager you can concentrate on the following things:

1. What style is taught there and how does it differ from other styles? This is not a question of superior or inferior styles but which one will cater to your needs most properly. For instance, if you are a good soccer player you may want to study a style that relies heavily on kicking. A wrestler may want to learn Judo or Aikido. Different people function best in different styles.

2. What percentage of the study group is young people? How does the teacher feel about them? It is as simple as that. Some people feel comfortable with young people, others do not.

3. How much does it cost and for what? The price itself is meaningless except in relation to what one gets. Two schools may charge the same and yet one may be open only three or four hours a week while the other has classes every day *and* gives private lessons.

Remember, make a wise decision, because once you have picked a school, you should stick with it until you have mastered the basics.

A FINAL BOW

The martial arts are a unique human achievement. It combines dance, self-defense, exercise, sport, philosophy, and a number of other human arts. As the saying goes, "You can study for three life times without seeing an end to it." Everyone who practices a martial art has his or her favorite aspect. For me the interesting thing about the art is that it is martial; that it came out of war and fighting. And yet, through the magic of human concern, it became something else that is wider and fuller and more important.

If you understand a style, any style, there will be two major stumbling blocks. First, there will be the "outsiders," the people who think of this art as only violent and about violence. Patience and explanation will eventually win them over. Secondly, inside the art there will be people who like to compare. They will compare this style to that form and this technique to that method. They have forgotten the whole point of the art—to "put everything together." While the problem is different with these people, its cure is the same—patience and explanation. If you can keep to these, you are mastering the "Kung Fu" of life.

—Ted Mancuso